~ Good Grief ~

*Finding Gifts in the Grief
of Losing a Child*

by

SARAH CHURCH

Copyright © 2012 by Sarah Church

ISBN 978-0-7414-7528-2 Paperback
ISBN 978-0-7414-7529-9 eBook

Printed in the United States of America

Published June 2012

INFINITY PUBLISHING
1094 New DeHaven Street, Suite 100
West Conshohocken, PA 19428-2713
Toll-free (877) BUY BOOK
Local Phone (610) 941-9999
Fax (610) 941-9959
Info@buybooksontheweb.com
www.buybooksontheweb.com

Dedicated with my love to Bryan's sisters

Kathleen and Peggy

~ Acknowledgments ~

I attempted to write this book many times over the last twenty years and each time, I balked and put it down, sometimes into the circular file. The results lacked. Either they were too maudlin, too angry, too depressing, or too unrealistic. It wasn't until I became a part of a writer's group that everything came together and I received the encouragement and support to finish my story. I am ever grateful and wish to recognize Jude Boardman, Judi Burwell, Mary Martin, and Charon Scott-Goldman, the women who enthusiastically urged me on and always wanted to hear the next chapter. I was also motivated to move forward with this project by my long-time good friend and poet Linda Goodman Robiner. I am also indebted to Tom Nicolino for his photographic know-how and assistance in refining the photographs in this book and to Carol Ellis whose grammar and spelling editing skills were invaluable. Last but most certainly not least, I extend my sincere thanks and deep appreciation to Roger J. Bass, Consultant and Partner of Resource Group 175, for his editorial review early on, his good advice, and his undying friendship.

~ Table of Contents ~

~ Preface ~

When I lost my twenty-one year old son Bryan in a drowning accident, I lost a piece of myself. Never in my wildest imagination did I ever entertain the thought of suffering such a loss, nor had I ever watched anyone close to me go through such a tragedy. I had no role models or lessons in how to heal. Not knowing how I was 'supposed' to behave allowed me to do what was right and natural for me - I cried when I needed to, I laughed when I wanted to, I swore if I felt like it, I slept until I could sleep no longer, and I sought help from those of my choosing. I grieved in my own way and in my own time. It's now more than a quarter of a century since that fateful day, and I'm finally ready to share my experience with others.

The day my son was born, my life changed. In a way, I was set free when he came into my life. I knew that somehow things were going to be different from that day on. Though I had grown up with two brothers, caring for and tending to my new baby boy gave me an ease and comfort with the male body that I'd never known before. It brought me a newfound sense of humor and made me a better lover to my husband. Remembering how my brothers were called Billy and Teddy even as adults and complained bitterly about it, I carefully chose a name for my son that couldn't be babyfied by adding a "y" to it. He was Bryan at age two and he was Bryan at twenty.

The day Bryan died, my life changed again. Everyday I think of all the parents who lose sons and daughters in the wars in Afghanistan and Iraq and all the mothers who fear for their children as they send them off to school. Every year, hundreds of parents lose their beloved children to suicide, illness or accidental death. A mother never gets over the loss of a child. None of us gets an opportunity to practice living with such a loss. It's thrust upon us unexpectedly. My experience is just one example of how one mother came to live with such a catastrophic loss and even found some gifts in the grief of that loss.

Today, I live happily with memories of my son who died a hero. Now I look forward to, instead of dreading, all the anniversaries associated with him. Every year, I celebrate his birthday, his death day, Mother's Day and Christmas in unique and meaningful ways that help keep his generous spirit alive. Each year, the Bryan Lee Coyle Endowment Fund at Oakton Community College Foundation honors a young person in their second year of the Automotive Maintenance program with a scholarship. With that endowment, Bryan's name will go down in perpetuity and he will always be remembered.

I experienced solace, joy and strength as I committed these stories to paper and if they are of any support and help to others, then I am doubly blessed for having told them. These stories are my tribute to Bryan and his all too brief, but well lived life.

~ Chapter One ~

The Beach Party
July 1983

The grating din of the door buzzer woke me that morning. I rolled over and squinted at the bright green numbers on the clock radio. It was 5:30 am. Quickly calculating the brief four hours since I had crawled into bed, I sighed aloud, "Damn, who the hell could that be?" I had planned to sleep in late that morning. Persistently, it rang a second time. I reluctantly hauled myself out of bed and staggered into the front room of my condo. Pressing the button and through a yawn I answered it. "Who's there?"

A deep male voice came over the scratchy speaker. "This is Officer Jamison from the Evanston Police Department. Could Officer Stuart and I please come up?"

"Oh, God, what's he done now?" I immediately thought.

My son Bryan and I had been through a lot over the past six years. I'd bailed him out when he rolled his car, went to get him in the middle of the night when he was picked up for hitchhiking, and even accompanied him to the suburban police station late one night to talk with officers about a gun that they were trying to find and get off the streets and out of the hands of young people.

However in the last three years, everything had been so pleasant, so normal and comfortable for both of us. At twenty-one years old, he had a good job as a mechanic at the local Shell station. He was enrolled in Oakton Community College and was living alone in his own apartment. He even

1

had a nice steady girlfriend. His life was turning around and no one deserved it more than he.

"Could he possibly have blown all that now?" I wondered.

I buzzed the two of them into the downstairs hall and went back to the bedroom where I threw on a robe, slipped into my moccasins and returned to open my front door. There stood two city cops in full uniform. One of them was at least six feet-two, balding and built like a prizefighter. He cradled his hat in one arm and held a clipboard in the other. His partner was a woman, much shorter and somewhat slight in stature. Her well-pressed uniform fit her perfectly, and she stood very erect accentuating her noticeably well-toned physique. Her hair was pulled back from her face more like a librarian than a cop. She had a very serious look on her face and spoke first.

"Mrs. Coyle, you'd better sit down. We have something to tell you." She entered the room and continued, "There's been an accident down at Lighthouse Beach and they haven't been able to locate your son, Bryan."

As I backed up and grabbed the arm of my sofa to lower myself into it, I merely stared at both of them. I eased myself slowly into the corner of my loveseat.

"What do you mean, you can't locate him? He's a strong swimmer. He's on the shore somewhere. Wait a minute," I said as I tried to stand up, "I'll throw some clothes on and I can go down there to help." The words spewed out of me like an erupting volcano. Then suddenly my whole body went hot. My heart was beating so hard and fast I was certain they could hear it.

I sat back down and blurted out, "I told him so many times how fickle Lake Michigan was. One minute it's calm and the next - stormy. Why didn't he listen to me?" By now, I was pounding my fist on the arm of the sofa and with a crescendo in my voice I all but screamed, "Damn it, damn him, damn that lake."

My tears were streaming and I was trying to get up but she had her hand on my shoulder and was pleading with me, "No, Mrs. Coyle, you don't have go down there. You shouldn't go there now." Both officers just kept repeating, "Is there someone we can call?"

"Someone we can call?" I puzzled, "No. There's no one to call. Bryan's father lives hundreds of miles from here with his new wife. My brother is vacationing in New York City with his wife. And my sister is away on vacation also." Then I added, "For God's sake don't call my mother."

"Do you have a friend we could call?" She continued.

"A friend?" I repeated, "Yes, I have a friend. I have two friends - Jack and his sister Janet. Call Jack. He'll come over."

Two days later, the following appeared in the Chicago Tribune:

Bryan Lee Coyle, 21, an Oakton Community College student and a certified auto mechanic, tried to help people, whether by stopping along the highway when he saw a car broken down or by jumping into Lake Michigan when a companion was drowning. He died Wednesday morning off the breakwater at Lighthouse Beach in Evanston in an attempt to rescue a friend struggling in 3-foot waves.

Bryan was atop the breakwater helping to hoist others up when he heard his name and a frenetic call for help at the end of the barrier. Without hesitating, he ran to the end of the breakwater and jumped in to help John, his friend. Later that evening, John told me that he and Bryan together submerged into the rough waters and came up out of them three times. The third time he felt Bryan give him a big push and, when next he landed, he was on the rocks and able to make it into shore safely. The following morning, the rescue team of divers found Bryan anchored in the sand at the bottom and when they pulled him from the water, one of his heavy combat boots was unlaced as though he was trying to get them off.

Even now, more than twenty years later, I regret that I did not follow my instincts and go to the beach that day. I know it would have been heart wrenching, but I also believe that had I been able to hold Bryan in my arms, I would have realized that his spirit was no longer inside that handsome well-formed body, but had gone to a better place. Going to the beach that morning would have helped me accept the reality of what had happened a lot sooner than I did. Instead, I was able to fool myself and pretend he was alive somewhere and I would see him again some day.

~ Chapter Two ~

Tough Love
July 1980

It was a Friday and I had had a particularly difficult week. As Executive Director of the Fine Arts Music Foundation in Chicago, the buck stopped with me. The board was upset over the cancellation of the pianist for the season's opening concert, the program notes would have to be rewritten, and the printer had called to say the brochures would be late. The only good thing at the moment was that it was six p.m. and I was driving home with a double martini in a paper cup next to me.

I was thinking, "I hope Bryan kept his word and got the leaves raked up in time for the trash." I pulled up in front of the house just in time to see Bryan dash out the side door, hop into his truck and take off.

"Damn it," I said to myself, "he didn't even rake the front." I picked up the mail from the box and, as I walked in the door and set my briefcase down, I couldn't help but notice a large package on the bench in the hall. It didn't take long to recognize that it was at least two pounds of marijuana neatly bound up in a plastic bag.

Leafing through the mail, I singled out and anxiously ripped open a letter from Evanston High School where Bryan was to begin his junior year in a month or so.

"Dear Parent of Bryan Lee Coyle: This is to inform you that Bryan was absent more than 30 days of his last semester and did not submit the necessary work to

5

*complete his sophomore year. As a result, he will not be
registered for the coming year."*

I set the letter down and went into the kitchen, opened
the cupboard and cradled the bottles of gin and vermouth in
my left arm while I grabbed the cocktail shaker with the
other. I mixed a double martini and, as I was gently coaxing
the last few drops from the shaker, I thought, "That's it! I'm
not putting up with this any longer. He had stopped going to
school, didn't have a job and was obviously dealing pot."

Four months earlier his father, my ex husband, had
begun sending him the child support checks directly. I knew
it was a mistake to give him several hundred dollars each
month and I told his father that it was the same as handing
him a loaded gun but he didn't agree with me. I also knew
that Bryan would be getting those checks for the next nine
months, until he was eighteen years old. It wouldn't have
done me any good to take my ex back to court with less than
a year left for me to receive child support. However, it may
have made a difference to Bryan had I done so. I'll never
know.

I'd made up my mind. I was not putting up with his
shenanigans any longer. I also knew it would take all my
strength to do what I needed to do. So, that evening I
fortified myself with a few extra straight scotches to build up
my courage and decided that when Bryan came home, I
would give him an ultimatum. I think it's called "Tough
Love."

He tiptoed in very late that night and found me in the
dining room waiting. Holding it an arms' length in front of
me, I confronted him with the package I'd found and
scolding him said, "Bryan, I'm very upset with you. To live
in my house and eat my food, you must either get back into
school or get a full time job. Otherwise, you are out of here.
I'll give you three months to make some changes."

Just like a typical teenager, he blew me off with a perfunctory, "Whatever, Mom!"

He picked up his package of pot and started for the stairs to the basement. I followed him, stopping at the top of the stairs. My voice escalating, I continued enumerating all the reasons why I was doing this, "You have to stop this, Bryan. You're going to get in trouble with the law. Time is running out for you and you won't be able to do anything worthwhile without a high school diploma. Think about it!" It appeared as if he was totally unconcerned because within minutes I could hear blasts of loud music from Led Zeppelin wafting up from the basement. I closed the door and went upstairs to my bedroom.

Twelve weeks later, on October 1, because there was no change on Bryan's part, I locked the doors to him. It was one of the hardest things I've ever done in my life. He sponged off a few friends until those mothers got tired of it and then he slept in his van parked anywhere that he legally could, in parking lots, on side streets and even in alleys. That lasted for several weeks.

This "Tough Love" thing sucks. My maternal instincts were to care for and protect him. He was my youngest and my only boy. I paced the floors at night when I couldn't sleep and I remember reciting out loud, "I know he can figure this out. A hundred years ago, a boy of seventeen was considered a man. He's got to be a man now. I know he can do it."

For weeks, every other day or so, Bryan would show up at the front door. "Can I come in and at least take a shower?" he'd ask. Sometimes he had a bag of laundry in his arms. I'd open the door and allow him in but at the same time, tell him in as stern a voice as I could muster something like, "Yes, you can take a shower and wash your clothes and then you have to leave again." I guess, as his mother, I never really want to completely cut the apron strings. Down deep I wanted him to know I believed in him.

With Bryan gone from the house though, I must admit that much of the time I felt relief. I thought, "What I don't know won't hurt me." Or, "Now, there's no one around to carp at me when I fix my double martinis each night or sit up until the wee hours sipping scotch until my eyelids won't stay open any longer. I can do as I please, eat when I want, watch the programs I want to see, and play the music I want to hear."

I'm not certain if it was out of guilt or selfishness or just plain addiction, but my consumption of alcohol escalated exponentially and within a few months, I was drinking in my office, drinking in my car, drinking alone at home, drinking whenever and wherever I could. My job was in jeopardy, my health was deteriorating, and I was hungry, angry, lonely and tired all the time.

My whole life was a mess, but that was all about to change.

~ Chapter Three ~

Step One
January 1980

It was ten o'clock on a sunny February morning and I was sitting in a local bar. The place was packed and every table was occupied. Timidly, I raised my hand and with a pounding in my chest I said, "Good morning, my name is Sarah, and I'm an alcoholic." It had taken me thirty-some Alcoholics Anonymous meetings in as many days to finally muster the courage and humility to utter those words aloud to others.

The fellow sitting next to me looked up from the New York Times on his lap, lowered his half glasses down to the tip of his nose and peered over the tops of them. He leaned over and whispered, "It's about time, Sarah. Ya' know no one has ever walked through those doors by mistake." Forcing an uncomfortable smile, I gave a little shrug and nodded my head.

There I was in a barroom full of people from all backgrounds, men and women, young and old, black and white, well off and poor. The morning sun sneaked in through the English basement windows at sidewalk level, creating rainbow streaks across the ceiling. The real focal point of the room though, was a highly polished oak bar curved at each end with sturdy pedestal stools and a brass rail on which to rest one's feet. Behind the bar were shelves top to bottom filled with every kind of booze you can imagine and backed with a mirrored wall making all that liquor appear to be twice as much. How ironic! There I was, comfortable and appreciating the real beauty of a barroom, and I wasn't even going to order a drink. Every table in the room was set with a pot of coffee, paper cups and a bowl of hard candy, all of which would be empty by the end of the meeting.

It was there in that meeting, among friends and strangers that I realized I had finally found, after years of searching, a place where I truly belonged. These people understood me and felt exactly like I did. They wouldn't judge or criticize me and they were willing to listen to me when I needed to be heard.

For the most part, I had not really seen or talked with Bryan in the past thirty days or so.

It was serendipitous that the topic of the morning was *"How Our Alcoholism Affected Our Families, Friends and Colleagues."* I didn't utter a word, but I listened carefully to everything that was said, and by the end of the meeting I knew it was time for me to go see my son.

I had been so wrapped up in myself that first month trying to get sober that I was totally unaware that Bryan also was busy changing his life. In less than three months, he had reenrolled in night school at the high school, had secured a part-time job at the neighborhood Shell station and had found two Northwestern University students who needed a third roommate in their five-room flat.

It was around noon when I backed my car into the last space on his block. I was nervous as I stepped out of the driver's side and walked to the front door of the three-story brick walkup and rang the bell. A young man answered and I asked, "Is Bryan Coyle here? I'm his mother."

This tall, clean cut looking young man dressed in blue jeans and an NU sweat shirt opened the door all the way, motioning me inside, and said, "He's still sleeping but if you wanna' wake him, his room is down the hall, second door on the right."

I walked down the dark hallway, stepping over a pile of clothes half way and gently rapped on his door, turning the handle at the same time and opening it a crack. Bryan was nestled under the covers and barely opened one eye to see who was there. "Mom, what are doing here?" he said as he recognized me, "What time is it?"

I sat down on the end of his bed and removed my gloves, laying them beside me. "Bryan, it's after twelve noon. I want you to wake up now." I said. "I have something to tell you."

He pulled himself up and leaned against the wall, propping a pillow for his back. He was naked from the waist up and I looked at his lovely masculine physique with his broad shoulders, well developed biceps and rippled abs thinking to myself, "What a beautiful young man you have grown into."

Once I saw that I had his attention, looking down at my feet, I began with, "Bryan, I haven't had a drink in over a month now. I've been going to AA meetings every day, sometimes more than once." Then I looked up at him. His face lit up like he'd seen fireworks on the fourth of July. That wide-eyed look on his face with that crooked smile of his is implanted in my brain forever. It was the same look that he had one Christmas morning when he came down stairs at eight years old and saw the electric train that Santa had brought, all set up and running under the tree.

"Oh, Mom," he said, "don't you remember me telling you that I thought you were an alcoholic?" I was so taken back by that remark that it took me a moment before I could answer him. "No, Bryan, I don't remember that whatsoever. I must have been in a blackout." Fighting the tears that were welling up, I continued, "I'm so sorry, Honey. You must have been so lonely and so scared. I'm so sorry you had to go through that for such a long time." He merely looked at me, not saying a word but smiling his crooked smile and looking so very happy. Before I left, I hugged my son, gave him a big kiss on the cheek and whispered in his ear, "I'm so proud of you, Bryan, and I love you so much. It's going to be a new day for you and me."

I left that morning with a much lighter load on my shoulders and as I closed Bryan's front door and walked to my car, I was grateful for the gift of sobriety. Little did I realize that my work was just beginning? A long difficult road lay ahead for me and I was in for some tough times if I was going to clean up all the wreckage from my past.

~ Chapter Four ~

Highs and Lows

Sobriety brought many challenges. The exaggerated highs and lows early on made my life exciting at times and depressingly difficult at others.

I really never wanted to return to the Chicago area after my divorce but the opportunity to work in the field of music and have a good salary for doing it lured me back. I loved the job that brought me back to Chicago from Ohio, but I soon realized that because of my drinking, I had damaged too many relationships and could no longer be very effective as the director. Reluctantly and sadly, I resigned one year after I stopped drinking and I immediately began a new job directing the National Alumni programs for the University of Chicago.

My mother, brother and sister denied my alcoholism, calling it another one of my indulgent fads. My relationship with my mother had always been difficult at best. She never approved of the way I raised my children always telling me how sorry I would be for trying to be so "honest" with them. It was fortunate that I chose to live miles away from her while I was a young wife and mother. Her preference was that I not bring them to her home until they were out of diapers. She and I were so different. She was conservative and I was liberal. She saw the glass half empty and I saw it half full. When I was growing up, she made all my choices for me. She chose my clothes, she fixed my hair, she decorated my room, and she even chose my college and my course of study. Some would say that she even chose my first husband also.

Out of duty and as her daughter, I would have dinner with my mother once a week. On one occasion early in my sobriety, my mother, who didn't drink at all, ordered me a dry martini and had it on our table before I was even seated. I had dropped her off at the front door and was parking the car while she secured the table. When I arrived and noticed it, wide-eyed I asked, "Mother, why on earth would you do such a thing when you know I'm trying to give up drinking?"

She answered, "I know, dear, that when you were drinking, you had many problems, but you were better then." What she really meant was, "When you were drinking, I could control you and now I can't." She was right and for the first time in my life I wanted something more than to please my mother. I wanted a sober life.

I had begun to feel more control over my own life. I started to really hear what others said, and I realized that their feelings and ideas were just as valid and important as how I felt or what I thought. My appetite improved because food tasted better to me, and I even lost some weight that I no longer needed. My graying skin began to turn pinkish again and I lost the puffiness under my eyes. A mere sunny day could make me feel good all over, and I could even remember all the events of the day before with clarity. However, the most important gift of all was that I got my sense of humor back and with it; I began to restore my relationship with Bryan.

Bryan came for supper every Sunday and always brought his laundry along with his happy humorous "grease monkey" self. He had shoulder length blond curly hair then and sparkly blue eyes. On his right cheek, there were six tiny light colored moles and if you looked closely, you could see they were in the shape of the big dipper. His sisters sometimes teased him unmercifully when he was little by calling him "Dipper Face." His crooked smile matched his generous nature and reflected his adventurous spirit. He had a swimmer's physique - broad shouldered, a muscular torso, slimming at the waist and straight well-shaped legs. His favorite clothes were well-worn T-shirts, blue jeans with holes in the knees and heavy combat boots.

I remember one time answering his knock on the door and opening it to see him standing there in a three-piece suit with a brand new haircut. I dashed for my camera and posed him proudly standing next to the piano, one hand resting on the lid. As I snapped his picture, I asked, "Bryan, you look wonderful, where are you going?"

He simply grinned at me, "Mom, I just did it for you." He said.

My response was immediate and enthusiastic. "Bryan dear, you've just erased every wrong doing that you ever committed. I love you."

Often, I would visit Bryan at the gas station late on Fridays and kibitz with him while he would close up the place and balance the cash register. I was certain that someday I would be helping him own his own automobile shop.

He told me once, "Mom, I have an idea for a business. I could fix cars for senior citizens and in exchange they would agree to "will" me the car when they die." Seeing a puzzled look on my face, he continued, "Don't you see, Mom? If I'm gonna' own the car someday, they could be sure I would take good care of it while they are still using it. It's would be a win-win."

This was the boy who at age ten, trudged up the driveway pulling his red flyer wagon loaded with an old lawnmower engine and told me, "Mom, when I grow up I'm gonna' build the car engine that cleans the air." He spent that winter in the garage dismantling that engine and putting it back together, over and over and over again.

Bryan received his high school diploma in the spring of 1981 and immediately enrolled in the Oakton Community

College automotive program. He successfully completed two years and was certified as a mechanic by the National Institute for Automotive Service Excellence.

The disease of alcoholism however, tends to run in families, and I could see that Bryan was using alcohol much the same way I had, to celebrate when things were good and to drown his sorrows when things weren't so good. I also knew he would have to discover all those lessons for himself. I bailed him out once when he rolled his car after a night of partying. His payback for that was not just to reimburse me the bail money but also to spend an hour with one of my friends from AA. That time, I asked Hal, a man who rode motorcycles and worked on cars, who started his drinking as a teenager, drank for many years and now had been sober for a long time. He generously gave Bryan more than an hour of his time over a cup of coffee.

We'd all like to think that as parents, we have a right to tell our children what they should and shouldn't do and that they will listen to us and take our advice. However, after most children reach a certain age, twelve or thirteen, they tend to rebel against such advice. When Bryan was in his late teens, all that was left to me was to demonstrate by the way I made changes in my life rather than to tell him how to change his. The pain of knowing what kind of an example I had set for my children when I was drinking was one of the most difficult mistakes for me to reconcile. The only way I could was one day at a time and with the help of others. When I look back now, it amazes me to remember that as I worked to make changes and improve my life, my children made changes in their lives also, and we weren't even all living together in the same town. Some would call that the miracle of sobriety.

~ Chapter Five ~

His Lost Puppy
March 1983

Chicago was in the throes of a mid-March cold snap and was waiting for another, hopefully the last, snowfall before the spring thaw. The air was cold, crisp and clear. In spite of all the city lights, I could see a sky crowded with stars. The night was beautiful and the air was still when the phone rang and Bryan's voice on the other end pleaded with me, "Mom, Kegger's lost and I'm afraid she might be in the water somewhere. Will you come help me look for her?"

Kegger was Bryan's puppy only six months old. I told him I'd come right away. I threw a sweater on over my pajamas and as I stepped into my boots, I pulled my parka from the closet and slipped an arm into it. Grabbing my keys from the table, I headed down to the garage. It was still dark outside. It was either the very beginning of a new day or the absolute end, depending on one's lifestyle. It was only a five-minute drive away and when I got there, Bryan was alone on the city beach calling out to Kegger.

The two of us ran back and forth on the sandy beach calling for her as Bryan explained, "We left my place about an hour ago to take a walk along the beach and all of sudden I couldn't find her." He continued, "Now, I'm afraid she may have fallen in off the end of the pier and couldn't make it back to shore."

We jogged up and down the shoreline several times, calling for her and finally my forty-seven year-old self couldn't keep pace with this twenty-one year-old bike-riding athlete any longer. Finally, I grabbed his arm and bending over to catch my breath, I gasped as I said, "Bryan, I have to sit down for a bit. I'm exhausted."

The two of us sat down on the pier, dangling our legs over the side. Bryan lit a cigarette and slowly exhaled that first delicious stream of smoke. For one brief moment, I wallowed in that glorious smell. I had quit that habit one year earlier after twenty-eight years of over indulging, but I still enjoyed the aroma of that first fresh wisp of new smoke.

In the quiet of the early morning, we could hear only the lap of the waves against the pilings and the gentle undertow of the water as it receded from the shore. Bryan was pensive and stared out toward the horizon. Breaking the silence, he turned to me and said, "Mom, if anything ever happens to me, just sprinkle my ashes over this lake."

I was a little stunned, and somewhat amused. With a little chuckle, I responded, "Sure, sure, honey and if anything happens to me, you do the same for me. O.K?" We agreed.

Four months later, I set Bryan free as I threw his ashes off the end of that very pier. My daughter Kathleen and her husband Tom were with me or I probably wouldn't have made it to the end of that pier. If I had, I might have jumped into the water along with his ashes. I was weak and despondent and so lost. I do remember vividly however, that when Bryan's beautiful silvery ashes were released over the calm waters of Lake Michigan that sunny day, my heart was unburdened from a heaviness it had been carrying around. I felt relief as though I also had been set free. Perhaps because I was fulfilling Bryan's wish or maybe because I knew that Bryan would suffer no more pain in this life, but had gone to a better place. When the three of us had finished our task, we stopped and bought double dip ice cream cones and sat in the waterfront park sharing our tears and stories about Bryan.

When he had finished his cigarette that March night four months earlier, I suggested that I drive him home and that he fix me a cup of coffee. He agreed and we left the beach not having found Kegger. Bryan didn't say a word all the way home. He simply stared out the passenger side of my car, his chin resting in the palm of his hand with a sad almost despondent look on his face.

There was no problem finding a place to park at that hour and I pulled up right in front of his building. The two of us got out of the car and as we neared the front door, we looked up and saw an animal's head with sparkly little eyes peering around the corner of the building. It was Kegger and she was coming from the alleyway. Her eyes had caught the street light beam and made her look like she was smiling. As the two of them noticed each other, they ran full speed toward one another. Kegger jumped into Bryan's arms and licked his cheeks and chin and nose and mouth. Bryan hugged her and then scolded her saying, "You scared the life out of me. I thought I'd lost you forever. Don't you ever do that again." Then he hugged her again, lowered her to the ground, patted her head and fastened her leash. "Come on girl, let's go home, you naughty dog."

Bryan's apartment was on the second floor and while he was brewing a pot of coffee in the kitchen, I suggested that I make myself useful by folding the clothes in the laundry basket sitting in the hallway. Bryan said, "You don't have to, but thanks." In my motherly fashion, I folded and stacked everything neatly at the foot of Bryan's bed and then I walked into the living-room. I plumped and fluffed the cushions of Bryan's secondhand tweed-covered sofa bed and sat down.

It was just getting light outside and that wonderful smell of freshly brewed Java wafted down the short hallway from the kitchen. Minutes later Bryan came into the room and with an apologetic chuckle he thanked me for picking up and handed me a mug of coffee. "Ya' know what, Mom?" He said. "Now, I realize what a parent goes through when their kid doesn't come home at night." I smiled and said, "Oh

Bryan, most people don't experience that feeling or learn that lesson until they're twice your age."

It seems as though Bryan learned so many of life's lessons at such an early age and accelerated pace. Neither of us really knew it at the time, but in the months ahead and much too soon in our lives, Bryan and I were to have experiences that would change us forever. We were to learn lessons that we would never forget.

~ Chapter Six ~

Did Bryan have a Premonition?

When I reminisce about the last few months before he died, I sometimes wonder if Bryan was readying himself, tying up all the loose ends of his life. I don't mean to imply in any way that he was suicidal. He was much too happy and well adjusted. I have wondered from time to time however, "Did he have some sort of premonition?"

April 8, 1983, was his twenty-first birthday and I had planned to take him to Milwaukee, Wisconsin, to tour the Harley Davidson motorcycle factory but they were closed that day so I had to give him a rain check. Instead I took him to the local Deli for lunch. He showed up wearing his favorite somewhat tattered "Harley Davidson" T-shirt and well-worn blue jeans with ripped pockets and holes in the knees. We ate Reuben sandwiches, coleslaw and chips and I bought him his first legal beer. It surely was not his first beer, but it was his first 'legal' one.

I whispered to the hostess as we were being seated that he was twenty-one years old today and when all the wait staff surrounded our table to sing in harmony *Happy Birthday,* Bryan blushed, smiled that crooked smile of his and looked at me as if to say, "Mom, how could you?" I loved every minute of that tease and only wished his sisters could have been with us. As the youngest in the family and being the only boy, he had learned well how to be teased and graciously enjoy it.

That evening, a few of us took him and one of his friends to Benihana. The oriental chefs tossing their knives in the air as they prepared our food right in front of us awed him. It was always fun to introduce Bryan to something new in his life. He embraced new experiences so willingly and enthusiastically.

For Mother's Day that year which happened to be Bryan's last one with me, he told me he would do anything that I wanted. I asked him to go to brunch with me and his grandmother, aunts, uncles and cousins (my mother, brother and sister and their families). He willingly agreed, wore his three-piece suit and even extended himself to assist his less than agile and very overweight grandmother out of the car and into the restaurant by offering her his arm. It was disheartening when she rebuffed him in her insensitive way. She never could see past the grease under Bryan's nails or his shoulder length blond curls to know the generous young man who only wanted to help by servicing and repairing her green Cadillac car.

It was not an easy outing for Bryan; rather it was more an ordeal. He told me once that he never felt he measured up to my family's standards. The truth is he more than lived up to them. He was kind, loving and loyal. Bless his kind heart. He went that day for me because it was Mother's Day.

My birthday falls in June, and to celebrate it when I was about to be forty-eight years old, Bryan invited me to go dirt-bike riding with him. We loaded his bright yellow Yamaha dirt bike onto the back of his red truck and off we went to the outskirts of town. About twenty minutes later we were parking the truck in a makeshift parking lot of packed dirt and I could see hills and dales of sand-laden earth for what seemed like miles. There were no trees to speak of, merely sagebrush like plants scattered about on the sides of the carved out trails. With trepidation, I climbed behind Bryan on the enormous seat of that huge bike and hugged my arms around his waist, anchoring my feet on the platform below. What came next was a roller coaster ride as we bounded up and down the dunes of sand and dirt. One ride was enough for me so I dismounted and took photos of his rides that followed. It was as if he might be saying, "Look, Ma, no hands!" He performed for me, doing wheelies and jumps and while I probably said something like, "Be careful, Bryan." Or, "That's enough now," down deep I was impressed with his athleticism and the ease with which he handled that big bike. I also understood a little better why he spent so much time lovingly dismantling and cleaning that bike so thoroughly after each time he rode it. On my shelf above my writing table, I have a miniature Yamaha motorcycle to remind me of that birthday when Bryan gave me a day of fun and sun and wind in my hair together with a piece of himself.

On July 4th, Evanston always had an extravagant parade with floats and queens and clowns tossing candy to the kiddies along the way. Bryan had always wanted to be in that parade and yet had never succeeded to make it happen. It was a gorgeous hot eighty-degree day with not a cloud in the sky. I, with several of my friends, found an ideal spot to stand and watch the parade. I was telling my cohorts about Bryan wanting to someday be in The Parade when I looked up at what appeared to be the very last float. There he was, standing tall in the back of his truck, shirtless and tanned, his chest and back painted red white and blue. He was proudly flexing his muscles and bowing to the crowd. We along with many of his friends who were standing on a rooftop near by, urged him on with encouraging salutes and yells. He got his wish to be in the July 4th parade and though we didn't know it then, it would be the last chance he'd ever have to do that.

On several occasions, I had reminded Bryan that he had promised to fix the minor dent in the fender of my car. After Sunday supper together on July 17, he took my car with him and told me, "Mom, I'll need two days to do the work and I'll finish it and leave it parked in front of my place so you can come and get it on Wednesday." I agreed.

On Tuesday afternoon, Bryan called and asked if he could use my car to go to a party that night. I pleaded with him saying, "Bryan, you are not insured to drive my car and if anything happens, I could lose everything. Please don't do it." He said he wouldn't and he didn't. He drove his truck.

That was our last conversation. My son-in-law picked my car up from the front of Bryan's apartment two days later. He had repaired the dent and the fender looked like new.

His friends who were with him that fateful night all went back to his apartment after the police arrived at the beach and finished questioning them. The group spent the rest of the night in Bryan's apartment, just talking and being together to console each other. They told me that when they arrived there, the entire apartment was all cleaned up. There was not so much as a dirty ashtray or a dirty dish in sight. The bed was made, all his clothes were either neatly hung up or put away in drawers and Kegger, his dog, was asleep on top of his bed. They said to me, "Mrs. Coyle, it was very spooky because it just wasn't what he would do. He wasn't a neat freak."

With all the memories of these last celebrations and incidences - his twenty-first birthday, Mother's day, my birthday, the fourth of July, the dent in my car, and his tidy apartment - I wonder, "Was Bryan becoming the responsible young man I always hoped he would be, or did he have a some sort of premonition?"

~ Chapter Seven ~

In Memory of a Hero
July 23, 1983

It was ten o'clock on a Saturday morning and there I stood in my bra and panties in front of a closet full of clothes all limp and neatly hanging from their wire necks. "What in the hell does a mother wear to her son's funeral?" I thought. "Not black. Bryan wouldn't want me to wear black."

Pushing the hangers from one side to the other, I checked out each outfit and finally chose a bright Kelly green cotton dress with an elasticized waist and cloth belt. All it needed was a piece of jewelry around my neck and then I could drape a sweater around my shoulders in case I felt cold. I mustn't forget my sunglasses.

My daughter Kathleen and her husband Tom had flown in from Seattle and her sister Peggy brought her boyfriend Mark by car from Ohio. Bryan's Dad and his wife came from Nashville, Tennessee, and my brother and sister along with their spouses had returned home, cutting their trips short.

My mother lived in town less than two miles from me and she would be there. Unfortunately my older brother who lived in Austin, Texas, and my older sister who lived at the foothills of the Cascades outside of Seattle, were unable to be there. I remember wanting all of them to know what a wonderful young man my son was and how much he cared about family. My second family, my ex-husband and two daughters, had their own grief with which to deal, so I turned to my many friends in AA who willingly supported me and who filled so many of the emotional needs I had. They were my family at that time.

We gathered at the funeral home at 2:00 p.m. I insisted that my ex-husband be seated with me, Kathleen and Peggy. We sat in the front row of the anteroom at right angles to the main chamber. More than two hundred and fifty young people showed up to mourn, pay tribute to someone they loved and offer their respect and condolences. I remember the entire front row filled with young women, all dressed to the nines and hairdos to match. There was no casket, but I remember my daughters asking me which clothes they should give to the funeral home for Bryan to wear. What did it matter? He was going to be cremated. I had tried to donate his organs. I knew it's what Bryan would have wanted, but they told me that his body had been in the water too long and all his organs had completely shut down. They wouldn't be able to use them.

Kathleen and Peggy together prepared a large poster board with selected photographs of Bryan's life and we placed it on an easel up front surrounded by three large outdoor plants and vases of wild flowers because Bryan loved the out-of-doors and the woods in particular. I remember the twentieth century parable by the contemporary American writer Richard Bach that David H, my actor friend from AA, read. It was a new twist on a very old biblical tale, a little story about a mechanic and his work.* I remember the music we taped and played. One of Bryan's friends, who had moved to California, wrote and dedicated a song for him. We played his tape and a medley of songs that included Led Zeppelin's "Stairway to Heaven," Kansas' "Dust in the Wind," and George Harrison's "My Sweet Lord." If I ever want a good cry to cleanse my soul, all I have to do is play any of those pieces. It's been twenty-some years since that day and I still am moved to tears when I hear that music.

---

* See Appendix

There was a reception that followed in a hotel across the street from the funeral home. I don't remember much about it.

The days that followed were long and sad. Jack, my good friend and lover stayed with me, held me when I slept, brought me coffee in bed in the morning and was "just there" for me, demanding nothing and offering everything. He was patient and kind and understanding. God bless Jack; he never asked anything from me that I couldn't give. He seemed to know just how fragile I was.

I slept for long periods of time when I could finally fall asleep. I lost my appetite, stopped eating and lost weight until a friend from AA who was an internist threatened to put me in the hospital if I didn't eat something. I ate.

Another friend from my AA home group came to see me several times a week those first few weeks. John D. is a psychiatrist and a good listener. He gave me wonderful advice. I remember he told me, "Those waves of grief that sweep over you spontaneously and unannounced should become farther and farther apart. If they don't, Sarah, you should see a counselor and address them head on." I was diligent and paid careful attention to all my many mood swings. The tsunami that had engulfed me did finally recede and became less violent waves of sadness and those waves eventually calmed and became further and further apart.

Grief is not neatly ordered. I never knew when the tears would come or when my grief would suck the wind out of me. I remember sitting at the dinner table in a restaurant with my brother, his wife, and my mother and all of a sudden I felt a huge knot in my throat and I couldn't breathe. I quickly excused myself from the group, dashed to the powder room and splashed water on my face. Realizing that I was alone in there, I sank to the floor on my knees and held my face in my hands and cried and cried. It all felt so hopeless, so empty and so final. There is no neat way to go through the five stages of grief - I denied it for months, I was enraged, I tried several times to strike a deal with God, I was depressed and then for short periods of time I would come to accept that which I couldn't change. It seemed as though all the stages of grief were mixed up together and even when I felt that I had reached acceptance, all of a sudden I found myself angry at God again or depressed or just willing to do anything to have Bryan back, to change the way things were, to get control over my life again. The stages and feelings of grief are all mixed up and come and go randomly for a long time, certainly the entire first year after such a shock.

I played my flute a great deal. I had always found solace and comfort in music and I am convinced that all those hours and years that I had spent practicing and playing helped me regain my ability to concentrate. I had always tried to teach my children that when you are at your lowest you should get out there and help someone else who is worse off than you. It was time for me to take my own advice.

I accepted a few musical engagements so that I had to make commitments to something or someone. I also volunteered at the local hospital as a runner. I would make deliveries of blood and urine samples to the lab for doctors and deliver flowers and gifts to patients. I was on a mission to get well. I forced myself to cook again. I continued to try to read books. I took long walks and I rode my bike with my good friends Jack and Janet. I went to AA meetings a lot.

In the late seventies, after a very painful divorce, I had run away from Ohio and my many good friends to return to Evanston, a place where I had grown up and with which I was familiar. I had accepted a very good job in Chicago, a city that I loved, and I lived less than a mile from the Great Lake Michigan. I knew those waters when they were calm and beautiful and I knew within minutes they could rage and become treacherous with storms. Unlike the ocean, Lake Michigan is unpredictable and fickle, but I loved it and so did Bryan.

Now, it had claimed my son's life and I found myself caught between loving it and despising it. Now, I had another decision to make. Could I continue to live near that incredible body of water and again find some peace in its beauty when it had stolen a piece of my heart and had taken my son from me? Should I leave it all behind and move on to something new? Should I run away again?

Bryan took me dirt bike riding for my forty-eighth birthday in June, 1983.

I understood why he spent so much time dismantling and cleaning his dirt bike.

When we moved to Akron, Bryan was three, Peggy was five &
Kathleen was eight.

It was fun to be around Bryan. He had a keen sense of humor, was courageous and brave, naughty and foolish at times, but always honest and loyal.

"Mom, I just did it for you."

Bryan receives his diploma in the spring of 1981

He slept in his van parked anywhere he legally could.

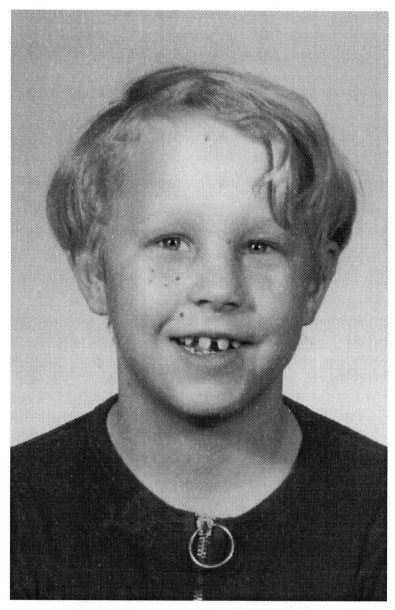

His sisters would call him "Dipper Face."

~ Chapter Eight ~

Running Away Again

Mother and I had just had a bite of lunch together in the dining room of her very upscale retirement home. With two choices on the menu that day, both of us chose the grilled cheese sandwiches. They were quite ordinary, made with white commercial bread and served with fresh raw carrots that had been shaved into curly cues on the side. A side dish of old fashioned fruit cocktail from a can upgraded a wee bit with one fresh strawberry accompanied the sandwich. For dessert we had pieces of cake that could have been eaten in two swallows and coffee that was weak enough to see the bottom of the cup on first sip. As I looked around the dining-room and saw all those older women adorned in their summer print dresses, thick stockings and neatly tied sturdy shoes, some even with purses draped over their arms, I was reminded how much I never wanted to end up in a place like that. Ordinarily, we would have gone out for lunch but the humidity made it too hot and sticky to bear and now here we were back in her comfortable air-cooled apartment.

She was seated in the fireside wing chair that had been in the family for at least fifty years. Newly upholstered, its elegant paisley wings cradled her shoulders and her cane rested along side her right leg. She looked every bit the granddame that she was. It was easy to envision the beautiful young woman I had seen in photographs. I studied her not so wrinkled face for a woman of eighty-two. I realized as her fourth born, I had only known her as a large, six foot tall, imposing and controlling figure in my life. As a child, I remember she was the one who made all my choices, what I wore, where I went, who I saw, and now even as an adult in my forties, she still had a great deal of control over me with her money and my need for help.

Mother was tapping her cane on the floor and talking on about my older sister. As always, she was complaining about something Carol's children had done or said. For no reason at all, one of those horrendous waves of grief engulfed me and I began to cry. At first quietly, but once the tears started, I had little control over their intensity. I lowered my face into my hands and sobbed out loud, "Oh, Mother, what on earth am I going to do now? He's gone. I'll never see him again."

"Oh, stop it, Sally!" she responded. Sally was a family nickname I'd been given as a little girl. "You're not the only one that has ever had this happen to her. Stop feeling so sorry for yourself."

Like I had been trained, I stopped. I got control, but I could still feel the lump in my throat and the pain in my chest. I raised my head and sat up, reached in my purse for a Kleenex and wiped my eyes of the smeared mascara, straightened my hair and crossed my legs, smoothing my skirt over my knees.

In as unemotional a voice as I could muster, I said, "Mom, Kathy called me from Seattle yesterday and asked me if I would come out there for a while. She's very lonely for family and she suggested that my spending some time near the mountains might help me heal a little more quickly. I'm seriously considering it. What do you think?"

She paused before answering, "Well, you know Dear, you can't run away from your problems. They go with you and if you go out there, I'll probably never see you again."

Sometimes, things simply fall into place making major decisions easier. I owned a condo and a friend of mine in the real estate business called that very week to tell me she had a client from Australia, a professor, who was coming to Northwestern on a six-week sabbatical to participate in a research project. He needed a furnished apartment and was willing to pay a more than reasonable rent.

Now I had to figure out how to arrange the travel. It was scary to think about driving across the country alone. On the other hand, it would be difficult to fly and take what I'd need for six months. I called my daughter Peggy in Ohio and invited her to make the trip with me. Happily, she accepted and I began planning.

I had to ready my apartment for someone else to live there, farming out my plants to friends and family and packing up certain valuables for storage at my sister's house. My real estate friend served as my manager in town and lastly I had to make sure my neighbors knew what was happening.

I went out and bought a carrier for the top of the car that looked like a huge McDonald's hamburger carton and I packed up my little red Toyota Corolla with the essentials of my life; my coffee pot, my typewriter (remember this was 1983), a few books, my camera, my bicycle, and my flute with some music paraphernalia. I left for Akron, Ohio, the last week in September to gather up Peggy and head west.

Peggy and I had not lived near one another for more than seven years at that point. After the divorce, Peggy at age sixteen or so, decided that she didn't want to leave Akron and all that was familiar to her so she remained there and lived with her father until she graduated. We had a lot to catch up on and in some ways our trip by car all the way out to Seattle gave us a chance to get to know one another in a whole new way. She was my rock so many times when I'd cry myself to sleep at night. She'll laughingly tell how I got sick in Cody Wyoming after we had lunch in a little diner and I can vividly remember the awful fight we had in Wall Drug store that ended up clearing the place out of all the cowboys and lumberjacks that were sitting around the bar.

The cold weather was setting in and the winter snows were beginning to arrive but we made it over the mountains in time and arrived at Kathy's house in Northeast Seattle on Wednesday, October 5, 1983.

~ Chapter Nine ~

My Visit with a Psychic
February 1984

I had no idea what to expect as I climbed into my car and followed the directions I'd been given to Dr. Mary Bacon's home. I guess I thought as a psychic, she would be exotically dressed and live in a mysterious, maybe even spooky place. Instead what I found was quite the ordinary neighborhood in Northeast Seattle. The house was a little two story cape cod planted right on the ground with virtually no foundation, like so many homes in Seattle. They appear to grow right out of the earth and hers was nestled among lovely flowerbeds.

I rang the doorbell and shifted from one foot to the other, having second thoughts about what I was doing. I had never seriously visited a legitimate psychic. I did allow someone to read the dregs of my left over tea in a Chinese restaurant once and I also paid a veil-draped swami to turn over tarot cards for me at a carnival years ago. Those times were just for fun. This was very serious. I was at my lowest. Now, I was drowning in sadness.

My friend Marilyn M. whom I'd met in AA referred Doctor Mary to me. I scoffed at the suggestion when she first mentioned it but then reaching a real low one-day and willing to do anything to feel better, I called Doctor Mary and set up an appointment. The phone call alone was surprising. As I began explaining who I was and where I was from, she interrupted me and bluntly said, "Don't tell me a thing about yourself." In her thick English brogue, she continued, "Simply bring a clean cassette tape with you and come to my house at one p.m. on Wednesday." As a child growing up in the forties, I had learned my manners well, so naturally I did as I was told and was very careful to be on time.

Doctor Mary was pleasingly plump and was all of four feet tall. She was between seventy-five and eighty years old and wore her white hair pulled back off her face into a loose bun on the crown of her head. She had the kindest eyes I've ever seen and to me she resembled the grandmother that I had as a child. I immediately felt at ease in her presence.

She invited me into her bookcase-walled den, and we seated ourselves across from one another, a small table in between with nothing on it but a tape recorder and a box of Kleenex.

She lowered her head, folded her hands in her lap and closed her eyes saying, "We'll start this with a prayer."

My heart sank. I thought, "Oh, no. Not a religious fanatic. I won't be able to stand it."

I had left my church more than ten years earlier. Suffice to say, I simply couldn't listen to anyone tell me to turn to God now. In one way, I felt God had let me down more than once. Doctor Mary stopped as abruptly as she had started, opened her eyes and said, "Oh my, they're telling me not to do this." She looked at me and asked, "My dear, do you feel like you are in a whirlpool?"

Somewhat irritated, I answered, "No, I don't."

She said, "Well, if you do, you can come up out of it, you know." Closing her eyes again, she continued, "My word, I see here a body of water, the bottom of which is golden and, oh, the current is so strong. Wait, there's something in the water. I see a young man, he's blond and he has the biggest smile on his face." Pointedly, she looked up at me and asked, "My dear, do you have a son who is giving you trouble?"

By this time I was completely weakened and I broke down and sobbed, my face cradled in the palms of my hands. "He's dead," I blurted out between my sobs. "He drowned."

Handing me a Kleenex, she gently asked, "Do you want to tell me about it?"

I answered, "My son drowned in Lake Michigan trying to help a friend. He was only twenty-one. He didn't deserve it. He was a good kid, trying to live his life the best he could."

"Well," she softly said, "there are some things he'd like you to know. Do you want to hear them?"

"Oh course, tell me."

"He wants you to know that he is perfectly satisfied with the way things are right now."

Then she continued, "You know, this young man had a very difficult life. There were things he wanted to do that he couldn't accomplish and they had to do with reading and writing."

I interrupted her here. and I said, "No one knew that except me." I went on to explain, "Bryan was diagnosed with mild dyslexia when he was a sophomore in high school. He had been passed along in school with Cs because he didn't cause trouble for anyone, but he never got the help that he needed. He told me once that he was embarrassed because he couldn't even write letters to his sisters." I went on with, "I tried to get him some help with a tutor but, by that point in his life, it was too late. He was sixteen and had other interests that took precedence."

I asked her if Bryan knew how much I loved him? She answered, "Of course he does." Adding, "And you should know that there are two gentlemen here with him. One is quite handsome and impeccably dressed and says he plans to watch over Bryan. Right now, that gentleman has his hand under your chin. Do you know who that might be?"

I'm sure it was my father telling me, "Chin up, Sally. I'll take care of Bryan. Everything will be all right."

The other man was Bryan's other grandfather, Hughie. Bryan had died on Hughie's birthday, July 20. I remember Doctor Mary saying, "Oh, yes, they'll often do that. It is strange how things happen sometimes."

She went on to tell me that she saw a much older woman way in the background who had a great deal of concern and love for me. I believe that was my grandmother who was one of the sweetest persons I've known in my entire life. Dr. Mary also told me she thought I'd stay out in the Northwest and probably work somewhere in education. In my long career in the not-for-profit sector, I've held positions at two schools along the way. Besides that, I was a volunteer one on one tutor for adult learners who couldn't read or write and I also taught private flute lessons.

When I left Doctor Mary's that day, I got in my car and thought, "I suppose I will come to intellectualize that visit in the future but for now I intend to hang on to all the things she said and take comfort in them."

The truth is I have never doubted for one minute the validity of that session. I have never tried to analyze it, question it, or dismiss it. It has stayed with me in times of sadness and in times of joy. I never felt the need to revisit Dr. Mary as a client but I did come to learn more about her background and how she came to that work.

I heard her tell her story one evening and she explained how as a child, she would hear things and see things that no one else could hear or see. It frightened her and she remained silent about it for years. When she was around forty years old, she was given the advice to pursue the development of her special gift and through that process, she learned that she was not only clairvoyant and clairaudient, but also could initiate a trancelike state to channel an ancient Chinese holy man who then would write through her in Chinese characters. She herself had no knowledge of the Chinese language. I witnessed that process one evening.

Doctor Mary returned to her native England several years later and I learned that she eventually died in the town in which she was born. I am ever grateful for our paths having crossed. She gave me the gift of opening my heart and my belief system long enough to have that last conversation with Bryan of which I was feeling so robbed.

I believe that when we open our minds to things that we don't completely understand, we open ourselves to others more completely. My daughter told me a story years later that she otherwise might not have, had I not shared my experience with her. This is her story.

Kathy had had one of those days when she could think of nothing else but Bryan and consequently, she was feeling very sad and lonely for him. As was her family's habit, that evening the four of them decided to go fishing at the Edmonds pier. When they arrived at the pier, it was crowded with people fishing who quickly told them, "They're really not biting tonight. We haven't caught a single thing all night."

Kathy found a spot out at the end of the pier away from the others and with no one next to her, she dropped her line into the water and whispered to herself, "Damn it, Bryan, if you're up there, put a fish on the end of this."

Within minutes, she felt a tug and started to pull her line up suspecting it was snagged on something, but as she reeled it in, there on the end was a very hearty rock cod. As she continued to remove it from the line, everyone gathered around her and one man asked, "What are you using for bait, there?"

When she told me the story, she laughingly said, "Mom, I couldn't tell them it was my brother." Was it her brother? Who knows?

Kathy's sister, Peggy, also tells a story about driving home very later one night after singing a gig in one of the clubs. The streets were deserted of people and it was raining hard. Her car began to make a terrible noise from underneath and she was sure it would soon stall out. She kept going, on a wing and a prayer as they say, and barely made it into her driveway. The following day as they began to tow it to the garage to be repaired, the mechanic told her, "Lady, you are one lucky driver. I'm surprised you made it home with this thing. The axel is about to drop off your car."

Peggy will tell you, "It was Bryan, I'm sure. He held that thing together long enough to get me home." Was it her brother? Who knows?

Mine is the best story of all however, because I like to say it's one that keeps on giving. Bryan is my parking angel. Everywhere I drive, I find a parking space right in front of my destination, every time. People have asked me to go along with them because they know they'll find a place to park. There is one incident though, that deserves telling in its entirety. On a busy Friday afternoon, my assistant and I were making a delivery up on Capitol Hill in Seattle and as we headed back to the office, Mary said, "Sarah, I wish we could stop for lunch. I'm hungry."

"We have time," I said. "Where would you like to go?"

"I'd love to go to Duke's up at the north end but we'll never find a place to park."

"No problem," I shrugged and up Broadway we continued. Just as I had predicted, right across from the entrance to Duke's was one spot on the street. I pulled in and hopped out of the car fishing in my purse for some quarters. As I began to feed the meter, I saw something shocking enough to beckon Mary to come back and see. Otherwise, no one would believe me. There on the meter above the coin slot was a decal in black Old English script that read, *"Sarah."* Was that Bryan's sense of humor? Who knows?

~ Chapter Ten ~

Surviving the First Year

There is no way to describe the first year after such a tragedy other than to call it pure hell. I hurt so badly physically and emotionally that at times I wasn't able to function. Born under the sign of Cancer, I tend to be a somewhat moody individual naturally, but my mood swings that first year were more exaggerated and intense than I've ever known.

Nothing was the way it was supposed to be. A mother is supposed to die before her child. I could find no rationale for the death of my child. I was not eating as I should have, I was angry with God, I felt so lonely and all I wanted to do was sleep all the time. I even reached the point at which I simply wanted to give up altogether and die myself.

Instead my instincts for survival kicked in and one of things I did was read a great deal, in short sittings because it was difficult to concentrate. I read everything from children's books about death to poetry about life and loss. I read self-help books on grieving and I kept a journal, several of them. When I look at those now, I see blurred tearstained pages, some of which don't make any sense at all.

When I arrived in Seattle, I stayed with my daughter and her husband and contributed to the household with my unemployment checks garnered from my work with the University of Chicago. I spent my days practicing my flute when I wasn't reading or going to AA meetings. I drove around the city learning where things were located and memorizing the one-way streets and short cuts on back roads.

One unseasonably warm and sunny afternoon I was driving in the University District and spotted a young man on the street clad in torn blue jeans but naked from the waist up. He was broad across the back and tanned to a golden bronze. His blond wavy hair fell on his shoulders and he was walking on the sidewalk with friends. I followed him for four blocks, careful to stay behind him. I was utterly convinced it was Bryan, he was alive, he had run away and hightailed it to the West coast. Eventually, I had to pass the group and saw clearly in my side mirror that it was indeed not my Bryan. I cried all the way home. Grief plays dirty tricks on us.

Six months after Bryan died, my unemployment was about to end and I was then forced into finding work. At the time, I felt very sorry for myself. Looking back now, I can see that it was ultimately a good thing, because I was forced into looking ahead instead of backward. AA teaches us that depression is when we are living in the past; anxiety is when we fear the future so the healthiest place to be living each day is in the present.

I mustered up the courage and energy to arrange for an interview for a part-time fundraising position with the Pike Market Medical Clinic. I was offered the job and at the dinner table that evening, I announced to my daughter and son-in-law, "Now that I have a job, it's time for me to move on, so I will be looking for a place of my own."

Things began to fall into place for me again. I rented a small two-room furnished apartment with carpeting I could sweep with a broom. The sofa was upholstered in scratchy green tweed and was so firm it forced whoever sat on it to sit up straight. The matching easy chair was anything but 'easy.' There was a one-person kitchen that was really just an alcove with miniature appliances. Boiling water on the stove would steam up the picture window in the living room and if I bought ice cream, I had to eat it all up immediately because the freezer was inadequate. The second room was a bedroom just big enough for a dresser and double bed. The bed was very firm and one of the most comfortable I've ever slept in. The bathroom was right off the bedroom, small but with a good shower and adequate shelf space. I grew to love that little place. My neighbors were all college students. It was right on the bus line which I used daily and a few steps from the Burke Gilman Trail, a popular place for biking & hiking. When I'd walk out my front door, the first thing I saw was Mount Rainier. That by itself gave me a different perspective on life. A half block away was the public bus stop making my commute to work easy and fun.

I couldn't have found a better place to begin working again. The doctors, nurses and staff at the Clinic were kind and gentle people. They were patient with me when I was vulnerable and pushed me just enough to get me back on track when I faltered. It was through their support that I was able to rejoin the outside world of working people.

I met Shirley at the Clinic. Shirley had a Master's Degree in Social Work and was one of the counselors who worked with our clients. I took an immediate liking to her. She had a calming peaceful quality about her and a common sense approach to problem solving. I began meeting with her and sharing my own personal struggles. She accepted me as one of her clients and in the many years that I have continued to work with her, I have learned a great deal about myself, about loss and about the power to heal. It was Shirley that taught me the importance of anniversaries in our lives. There were times when I would experience very strong feelings, either good or bad, and when I would stop to figure out what might have transpired on that day years earlier, many times I would come to realize it was the anniversary of something significant in my life. Shirley has given me much good advice and has always encouraged me to follow my instincts in the healing process.

One of those instincts was to get out and help others who were having a harder time than I. So I began to explore programs in the city that needed volunteers. I seriously considered volunteering in the Seattle Hospice program but found that it was the wrong time for me to do that work. It was too soon after Bryan's death. Instead, I became involved in the service program for AA and offered to participate in the Speaker's Bureau Program.

I signed up to speak at the local Junior High Schools, sharing my story about alcoholism and answering questions about the disease. I would begin all my talks with a question, "How many in here know someone, yourself, a friend, a relative, an acquaintance, who you believe has a problem with alcohol or drugs?" On every occasion nearly 100% of the young people would raise their hands. In AA we learn that our alcoholism directly affects the lives of at least seven people close to us. My question to those young people bore that out every time.

I would tell them my story and how I currently deal with my disease of alcoholism, a day at a time. I tried to answer their questions as honestly and sincerely as I could.

I always told those young people the story of my son's death and I ended all my talks with, "I will never know had Bryan not been drinking that fateful July night, whether he might have decided differently and removed those heavy combat boots before jumping into the rough waters of Lake Michigan to help save his friend, John."

It was also about that time when I trained for and began my volunteer work as a one on one tutor to illiterate adults. I worked with two young adults, Greg and Tracy, over the next four years. Neither could read nor write beyond the fourth grade level yet each was holding down a full time job.

Greg's boss recognized leadership qualities in him and enrolled him in the program. He wanted to be able to move him up in the company. Tracy, a mother with three children, was pretending to read her five-year old daughter a bedtime story one night and the child interrupted her with, "Mommy, that's not what it says."

Both were young adults who shared a history of being passed over in their public educational system just as Bryan had been overlooked. It's no surprise that I received more than I gave in that work. I felt an incredible closeness to my son as I helped others with disabilities like his. This was a huge step in my recovery. As a bonus, my relationship with the Literacy Center continued to evolve and eventually included a consulting contract, membership on their Board of Directors, Group Training opportunities and much more. To this day, I continue to support their programs to help adults who need it learn how to read and write.

~ Chapter Eleven ~

Memories

If Bryan were alive today, he would celebrate his fiftieth birthday on April 8, 2012. I can't begin to imagine what he would look like, where he'd be living, what his work would be. Would he be married? Would he have children? Would he have been in the service? I do carry a few vivid memories of Bryan's life but they stop abruptly at twenty-one years of age. The day he died.

John Waddell, an artist and sculptor, was commissioned to create a public art work in Phoenix, Arizona. Mr. Waddell was so emotionally moved by the untimely and tragic death of the four young teenage black girls killed in the church fire in Birmingham, Alabama, in 1963, that he chose to commemorate their lives with his commission. He recreated a life-size sculpture in bronze of those four girls dancing around a beautiful pool of water, not as teenagers but as young women, the ages they would have been had they lived. With that sculpture, John gave the parents of those girls an image to hold, an image of what the future could have been had their daughters lived to become young women.

As a little boy, Bryan was fun to be around. He had a keen sense of humor, was courageous and brave, naughty and foolish but always honest and loyal. He was my third child and born breach face up. He had two sisters, Kathie and Peggy, four and two years older than he. In his short life of twenty-one years, he took on the roles of both the baby of the family and the head of the house. When he was little, he was a cute towhead and took center stage, and we all catered to him until his kindergarten teacher pointed out to me how we were spoiling him. As he grew up to be a young teenager, too much was expected of him, and when his father left the family, twelve year-old Bryan tried to fill shoes that were way too big for him.

I remember when Bryan was a real little guy, maybe two months old, still waking in the middle of the night to be fed. Before waking me to feed Bryan, my husband used to get up and diaper him. He'd lay him on the bed next to me to change him. One night I was awakened by a spray of warm liquid in my face and I opened my eyes to a fountain of pee from this little penis right next to my head. Pat and I shared a laugh, I washed my face and after he was diapered, Bryan got fed and bedded down again until morning.

I remember when Bryan was about three years old, he was agile enough to climb the ladder of the next-door neighbor's slide and come down all by himself. One afternoon I was sharing a cup of coffee on my neighbor's porch and watching the activities in the yard. Little Bryan struggled up the ladder, seated himself at the top of the slide and yelled, "Look, Mom. Watch me slide down." Down he came and completely disappeared into the ground. Moments later in 'Kilroy' fashion, Bryan's little head peaked over the top of the ground and he cried out, "Someone, come get me outta' here." He was crying but as I look back, I'm certain it was his pride that was hurt more than his little pliable body.

David, my neighbor's seven-year old son, jumped up and down, made circles in the air and announced with much pride, "It worked! It worked! My elephant trap worked." David had dug a hole about two feet deep at the base of the slide and covered it with branches and leaves. I have no idea how he thought an elephant was going to get to the top of his slide to sail down into his trap. But it, indeed, worked for Bryan.

When we moved to Akron, Bryan was three and went to half-day nursery school to meet some new friends. The next year when he was four, I kept him home with me believing he would not then be bored when he started Kindergarten at five. We had a wonderful year together. Both girls were in school all day, and Bryan and I explored the city, played in the parks, walked the dog, shopped and cooked and cleaned together.

One afternoon we were looking for a hardware store to buy some paint to change the color of his room. He was in his car seat, unlike any you see today. In fact, a parent probably would be arrested today for endangering a child if he or she used the car seat we used for Bryan. I remember it had a plaid cloth seat, steel loops that went over the passenger seat of the car, and a miniature steering wheel attached to the steel rim in front. It was raised up from the car's seat so that Bryan could see out the windows just as well as I. The windows were rolled down to invite the fresh spring air in and all of a sudden, I heard Bryan say quite loudly, "Mom, Mom, look at the *fuck*. Look at the *fuck*." I gasped and turned my head to see a huge yellow semi 'truck' pulled up right next to us at the light. The construction worker at the wheel, his hardhat propped on the back of his head was laughing aloud and waving at Bryan. Then he winked at me and pulled away. I am happy to report that Bryan did lose his little speech impediment soon thereafter. It made for a good story over cocktails that evening.

When Bryan was eleven years old and in the sixth grade, I got a phone call from our neighborhood pharmacist. "Mrs. Coyle?" he started in, "I'm sorry to have to tell you that I caught Bryan taking a pack of pencils from the store this afternoon." I was dumbfounded and speechless. I asked him if I should come get him, but he went on to say, "With your permission, Mrs. Coyle, I'd like to handle it from here. I've already told Bryan that he'd have to sweep the alleyway behind the store to repay the cost of the pencils and he's out there working now." I gratefully thanked him for doing that and reassured him that I was certain that would make a much stronger impression on Bryan than anything I could have initiated.

I remember vividly the night that my husband left our house for good. Young twelve- year old Bryan took hold of my hand, looked up at me and said, "Mom, don't worry. I'll take care of things now." I didn't know if I should laugh or cry. I guess I did both.

Naturally, according to Murphy's Law "What can go wrong, will go wrong," and things began to break down around the house with regularity after Pat left. One evening, Bryan and one of his friends were attempting to fix a leaky faucet in the kitchen sink. The girls and I were sitting at the kitchen table watching and giving directions like backseat drivers. Bryan was under the sink on his back twisting a plumber's wrench round and round the main pipe. His friend Jake was in the basement waiting for the signal. Bryan finally relaxed his tool and yelled, "OK Jake, let 'er rip!"

The next thing we knew, water was everywhere, gushing out all over Bryan, all over the cupboard and all over the floor. Everyone screamed, Jake got the message, shut the valve down, and we all ran for towels to mop up the mess. The next day, after getting everyone off to school I phoned the plumber to come and fix the faucet.

The first Christmas after my husband Pat left the family was difficult in many ways. Bryan was thirteen years old and the children and I planned to invite anyone who had no other place to go for Christmas dinner. Kathy's friend, Edie, who would otherwise have been alone over the holidays, joined us. It was Christmas Eve and we were going to have dinner and open gifts. Peggy had stewed and fretted over what to get Bryan so I advocated for a pair of ice skates telling her he's always going over to Forest Lodge, the neighborhood ice skating pond, and I know he could use a new pair of skates. She bought him some. After all the presents were opened and the floor was a mess of wrappings, I noticed

Bryan wasn't around. I called out to see if he had left the house but he answered, "Be right there." A few moments later, there he stood in the doorway wearing over his jeans and shirt, a pair of pajamas that his Grandmother had sent. They had feet in them, were pale blue with a space ship design and they were at least two sizes too small. I had given him a helmet for his motorcycle that he was wearing and he had donned the skates that Peggy gave him. Unfortunately, none of us had a camera at hand for a photo, but in my mind's eye I can still see him plain as day.

When I became a single parent, not only did my life change, all three of my children had to readjust. I was no longer a stay-at-home mom and I think each of us expressed our anger at the situation in our own way. For Bryan, he changed his whole group of friends. Overnight it seemed, he no longer felt he fit in with youngsters from intact families. He began to run with a group that we called "street kids." Most of them really were not bad boys but with so little supervision and no strong role models in their lives, they were seemingly always on the edge of trouble. At the urging of Kathie, my oldest who was eighteen and beginning college at the time, I sold my house and Peggy, Bryan and I moved away to a duplex in Shaker Heights, a suburb of Cleveland, to try to begin a whole new life for ourselves. Peggy and Bryan had to readjust once again. They had to go to new schools, find new friends and learn their way around a new neighborhood. It wasn't easy on any of us. Peggy decided to return to Akron, live with her dad and finish her high school education there. One year later, Kathy, Bryan and I moved to the Chicago area and Bryan had to make more changes.

When Bryan was almost sixteen, he and I were living together in a little house in Evanston. Kathleen was traveling across the country with a friend and Peggy was in Akron. One evening, we had just finished supper and the two of us were seated next to one another on the sofa in the den. Out of the blue, Bryan turned to me and said, "Mom, there's something I have to tell you." Looking right into my eyes, he continued, "When we were living in Cleveland and I was in the eighth grade, remember when I went to a rock concert at Blossom Center one night? Well, after the concert I got separated from my friends so I decided to start hitchhiking. A man dressed in one of those blue lab technician coats picked me up and offered me a beer on the way home. Before I knew it, we were off the freeway and onto some God forsaken deserted road. He had a knife and he forced me to get out, take my clothes off and kneel on the ground. Then he raped me. I was so scared I didn't even have the sense to get his license number. All I could think of was, 'I'll never see my family again.' When he was done, he jumped in his car and left." After a tense silence, Bryan said, "Mom, how does that make you feel?"

My entire body was filled with red-hot rage. Without hesitation, I said, "Oh Bryan, if that man were standing here in front of me and I had a knife in my hand, I'd have no trouble whatsoever plunging that knife into his belly and twisting it." Then, I asked Bryan, "Have you carried that around all by yourself these last three years or have you been able to share that with anyone?" He said he hadn't told a soul. Then I asked, "Honey, why didn't you come to me?"

He answered, "Because, Mom, you always warned me about hitchhiking and also, I knew you'd make me go to the police." I had to admit to him he was right on both accounts.

Whenever Bryan would get in any trouble, I never wanted to believe he could land in jail because I feared what every Mother fears, that he would be raped and abused in there. My son never had to experience jail to know that horror. I still feel sad that he carried that burden all by himself all those years. I truly believe that we are only as sick as our secrets and I'd like to think that once Bryan told me his story, he began to heal from that painful ordeal. We never spoke of it again.

~ Chapter Twelve ~

The Sun Always Rises

Tomorrow is the anniversary of Bryan's death. Twenty-eight years ago I opened my door to that dreadful news. Tomorrow I plan to release twenty-eight red roses into the harbor waters outside my home on this island where I live. The current will carry them south to the open waters of Puget Sound and I will take a deep breath and try to imagine what Bryan would be doing if he had lived. "Building engines? Teaching children? Working out? Cracking jokes?" For certain, "Helping Others."

I'm not sure if time heals *all* wounds. I am sure that time has helped me learn how to live with the loss of my only son. Time helped me create a belief system to accept things I would never have thought possible. For example, one of my most difficult lessons in life has been how to "let go," and with Bryan's death, I've been given the ultimate challenge in learning that lesson. I always believed, but now I know with certainty that my children were only loaned to me; they did not belong to me. My job as their parent was to help them grow from babies into responsible, sensitive, giving adults who embrace life and live up to their greatest potential. Bryan did that and ended up giving the ultimate gift of his own life to help his friend. It's a choice he made as a loyal, sensitive, and giving adult. Whatever Bryan was here on earth to do, he accomplished in his brief twenty-one years. Now, it's my job to celebrate that life and allow him to move forward to do whatever it is that he needs to do. I must "let go." I do believe that the pain he endured in this life is now over for him and something better is in his path.

Some things are easier than others when it comes to living with the loss of a child. Early on, I found a way to deal with the many anniversaries of Bryan's life by celebrating them rather than dreading them. This forces me to use my imagination and when I do, it soothes the pain and eases the depression of looking backward to what used to be. Instead, I must look forward to things yet to come.

Each year on April 8, I celebrate Bryan's birthday. I always try to do something that I think would put that crooked smile on his face. One year I was in Gig Harbor shopping for the day with a good friend of mine. It was a lovely sunny April day with the smell of spring in the air. It was around three in the afternoon and as we were crossing the street, a boy about eleven years old was coming toward us from the opposite direction. He was by himself, studying the pavement intently as he toted his book-bag on his back, and whistled a little tune quietly to himself. Midway across the intersection, I stopped him briefly, handed him a twenty-dollar bill and said, "Have a great day. This is for you from Bryan." Then, I was on my way, not waiting for a reply.

When I turned around to look at him a second time, he was on the other side and had stopped dead in his tracks. He was staring at me, his mouth agape and eyes wide open. Holding the twenty in his hand, he slowly regained his trek. Mary Lou and I giggled with each other and she said, "Oh Sarah, can you just imagine what his mother will say when he goes home this afternoon and tells her, 'A lady stopped me on the street and gave me this.'"

I laughingly answered, "Oh, yeah, sure! And I have a bridge I'd like to sell you."

One year, I was in Shucks Auto Parts store buying new wipers for my car and on my out in the parking lot I spied a young man, grease up to his elbows with his head under the hood of his car. I walked right up to him, tapped him on the shoulder, handed him a $20 dollar bill and said, "Good Luck from Bryan. I hope you get it fixed."

Two years ago, on his birthday, my husband and I took ourselves uptown to the parking lot next to the town's fast food hamburger joint and we put five dollar bills folded inside little notes that read, 'Have a little fun on Bryan' under the windshield wipers of all the cars in the lot. Then we went into the restaurant, ordered our hamburgers and sat by the window to watch the fun. Several young people came in that night all excited wanting to tell all their friends about what they found only to then hear they weren't alone. I'm certain Bryan would have seen the humor in all of it. In all these ways over the many years he's been gone, I have gotten the gift of sharing Bryan's birthday with him through reaching out to others.

In 2008, twenty-five years after Bryan's death, I celebrated Mother's Day by placing a huge bouquet of red roses on the altar in the sanctuary of our church. There were forty-six flowers in all, one for each year he lived and one for each year that he'd been gone. As a part of the "Joys & Concerns" when the congregants ask for prayers for themselves and those they love, I offered a rose to every mother who was there, with the hope that they might receive the same joys that my son Bryan brought into my life when he was alive and the peace that I have found through the years he's been gone from this earth.

On the anniversaries of his death, I try to focus on the number of years he lived and the number of years he's been gone. Tomorrow, twenty-eight red roses, one for each year since his death, will float out to sea from the calm waters in Quartermaster Harbor to the deep ones of the beautiful Puget Sound.

At Christmas time, I concentrate on gifts for others, mostly children and young men. The "Giving Tree" at the holidays always has a gift under it for some child from Bryan. On Mother's Day, I try to remember other mothers with things like the flowers on the altar this past year or with something like a donation to Mothers Against Drunk Driving.

I know it is natural to feel guilt when someone close to us dies. I've let go of the guilt I felt for not being able to do everything right when I was raising Bryan. As a loving mother, I did the best I was able at the time, and I'm sure that my children knew it or have come to understand it. I believe they have forgotten and forgiven me for all the mistakes I made as their mother.

Even though some things get easier with time, there will always be difficult questions to answer. I am still somewhat uncomfortable when someone asks me, "Do you have children?" or, "How many children do you have?"

Should I answer, "I had three and now I have two?" or "I raised three children?"

Invariably, the next question is, "Where are they now?" That's the tough one. Here is an answer that I practiced and continue to use over and over. "I lost an adult son many years ago in a drowning accident and I have two daughters. One lives quite close by and is an artist. The other lives back in the Midwest and is a cabaret singer in Northeast Ohio."

I purposely deliver the sad part of that answer first and end with the information about my other two children. The one who asked me can choose to ignore a response to the death or they can more easily acknowledge their condolences with something simple like, "Oh, I'm so sorry to hear that."

Most people however, continue the conversation with a remark like, "Oh, how do you deal with such a horrible loss? I don't think I could ever get through it."

There are short retorts I could say like, "I do it a day at a time." Or, "Life isn't always fair, is it?" What I truly believe is something more like this. "None of us really knows how we will respond to the challenges and surprises with which we are faced. We all probably have hidden strengths that surface when we need them most. Mine did, and I'm very grateful for that."

My experience is that most people are rather uncomfortable talking about death or the loss of a child. There's a part of me that would love it if others, when they hear that news, had the courage to ask, "What was Bryan like?" Or, "Tell me about Bryan. How old was he when he died?"

One of the most difficult things about losing a child is the fear that they will disappear altogether, that everyone will forget them, that their life has no meaning, no significance. Nothing could be further from the truth. That child is with a mother always, every day, every hour. There are so many times and situations in which I find myself thinking, "I wonder what Bryan would say or do?" or "Bryan would love that." or "That would really make Bryan angry or happy or amused?"

Almost immediately after Bryan's death, I began making annual gifts to Oakton Community College in his name. After several years of this, the office of the Educational Foundation for the school came to me and asked if I would like to establish their first educational endowment and dedicate it to the school's Automobile Mechanics Program. I agreed and because of that, every year at least one and sometimes two deserving second year student(s) in the program receive money to buy the tools of their trade. With that endowment, Bryan's name will live in perpetuity and others like him will move forward in his honor.

One of the things I told my daughters soon after his death was that I wanted and needed so much to talk about him, tell stories about him, remember the times we were all together. I needed them to do that with me because they also knew him from the beginning. We still share our thoughts and feelings about Bryan and it gets easier and easier to do so. I believe that those conversations honor who he was in life.

I mentioned earlier that Bryan's death changed my life and one of the most profound changes came through my personal struggle with how I viewed death and dying and my own fear of dying. One of the gifts of my grief has been the change I experienced in that view. I no longer fear death. When I die, I will once again be with him. I have come to believe that we are born out of death and at the end of this life, we return to death. It is one enormous circle, life and death. Those who work with dying children tell us that children find it so much easier to die than we adults do. Steven Levine, in his book <u>Who Dies,</u> says that it was always the parents of dying children that he had to counsel. The children themselves were ready to embrace death but often times clung to life because their parents couldn't let go of them. Perhaps children, having lived fewer years are much closer to the whole transition from death to life and are consequently less afraid of it. The longer we live, the further from that part of the circle we travel.

I've not mentioned God in this whole process. I personally believe in a power far greater than myself, greater than any human being. Some call that power God. Some call it Nature or Higher Power. Whatever title one attaches to it is not important. Someone once told me they call it "Good Orderly Direction." The important thing is that we recognize that we are not all powerful, that we must succumb to powers much greater than ourselves. Nothing proves that more than the hurricane winds that blow, or the tornados that whirl, or the tsunamis that swallow up the earth. Nothing says it sweeter than the sun that rises every day and the seasons that change every year and the flowers that bloom or the seeds that burst forth into crops.

It's true. Each day is precious and life goes on, the sun will rise and the rains will occasionally fall and the sun always rises again.

~ Appendix ~

This is a modified version of a 20th Century parable that appears as a prologue to the book <u>Illusions</u> by the contemporary American writer, Richard Bach. We chose this as a reading at Bryan's Memorial Service.

There was a master come unto the earth, born in the land of Ohio, lived on the mystical shores of Lake Michigan. The Master learned of this world in the public schools of Illinois, and he grew in his trade as a mechanic of automobiles. He believed he had power to help himself and others and as he believed so it was for him to come to the aid of others.

The shops and garages where he worked became crowded and jammed with those who sought his help and his talent, and the streets outside, with those who longed only that the shadow of his passing might fall upon them, and change their lives.

A friend said to him, "A man has to work for his living in this world." Our mechanic replied, "Once there lived a village of creatures along the bottom of a great crystal lake. The current of the lake swept silently over them, young and old, rich and poor, good and evil. The current going its way, knowing only its own crystal self."

"Each person in his own manner clung tightly to the pilings and the rocks of the lake bottom, for clinging was their way of life, and resisting the current, which had been learned from birth."

"But one person said at last, 'I am tired of clinging, though I cannot see it with my eyes, I trust that the current

knows where it is going. I shall let it go and let it take me where it will. Clinging, I shall die of weariness.' And he surrendered to the current.

"Yet in time, as he refused to cling again, the current lifted him free from the bottom and he was bruised and hurt no more. But his friends wept and said, "Our friend!" All the while clinging to the rocks, and when they looked again he was gone, and they were left alone with his legend.

The friends and the family were silent. Not a voice, not a sound was heard upon the waves, across the shores where they stood. And the waves whispered against the silence. In the path of our happiness shall we find the learning for which we have chosen in this lifetime. So this is what we have learned this day, and chosen to leave you now to walk your own path as you please.

And our lost friend went his way, through the crowds, and left them, and he returned to another world of men and machines.

~ Bibliography ~

A Grief Observed by C.S. Lewis
Talking to Heaven by James Van Praagh
Closer to the Light by Melvin Morse M.D., with Paul Perry
The Healing Power of Humor by Allen Klein
Who Dies? by Stephen Levine
Live with Loss by Kate Walsh Slagle
Suicide and The Soul by James Hillman
When Someone Dies by Sharon Greenlee
The Fall of Freddie the Leaf by Leo Buscaglia
Paula by Isabel Allende
Gift from the Sea by Anne Morrow Lindbergh
Embracing Two Lives by Kathleen O'Conner

~ About the Author ~

Sarah Church is retired and lives with her husband on an island near Seattle. For more than twenty-five years, she served as a chief fundraising executive for several not-for-profit organizations in the Puget Sound region. In her work, she contributed to numerous professional publications. Good Grief is a memoir inspired by her successful recovery from the catastrophic death of her young adult son. It spans three years before and one year following his drowning accident. Many who have lost adult sons and daughters in the wars, through suicide, accidents or illnesses have found her story uplifting and inspirational.